Whispers In The Ink

Waking Verse

Subi Sheikh

India | USA | UK

Made with ❤ on the BookLeaf Publishing Platform
www.bookleafpub.in
www.bookleafpub.com

Dedication

This book is dedicated to my mother, whose unwavering support and encouragement have been my guiding light. Her presence has been a source of strength, and her belief in me has fueled my passion for writing. She was the first to hear my poetry, admire my words, and inspire me to write more. Every verse in these pages reflects her support, reminding me that dreams flourish in the warmth of those who stand by us.

I also dedicate this book to the citizens of India, hoping these verses awaken a deeper understanding of our society and the realities we often overlook. May these words serve as a mirror, urging us to recognize the challenges around us and embrace the responsibility of bringing positive change. It is time we rise above indifference, nurture hope, and work toward a future where kindness, justice, and unity lead the way.

Preface

"Poetry is when an emotion has found its thought and the thought has found words."
— Robert Frost

This collection of poems is a reflection of the world we live in—its dreams, struggles, and unspoken emotions. Each poem serves as a window into the soul of society, shedding light on themes that shape our lives yet often go unnoticed.

These poems are not just words; they are echoes of reality and dreams intertwined. If even a single verse stirs a thought, sparks a change, or lingers in your heart, then this journey of poetry has found its purpose.

— Subi Sheikh

Acknowledgements

All praise to the Creator, the source of words, wisdom, and the emotions that shape them into poetry. Without His guidance, these pages would be mere whispers lost to time.

To my family—you are the roots of my dreams, the hands that lift me, the love that fills every word I write. To my mentors and friends—your belief in me lit the way even when doubt clouded my path. To my readers—this book belongs to you as much as to me. If even a single verse lingers in your heart, my purpose is fulfilled.

A special thanks to BookLeaf Publishing—for not just giving writers a platform, but for keeping the soul of books alive in a digital world.

And finally, to the fleeting moments—the quiet, the chaotic, the forgotten, the profound. Thank you for whispering poetry into my soul and reminding me that stories are everywhere, waiting to be told.

With love and gratitude,
Subi Sheikh

1. A Dream For My Country

I want my country to be like this,
I want my country to live in bliss.
Where every person should care and share,
And every judgment should always be fair.

Where every religion should freely follow their faith,
And there should be no place for enemies or hate.
Where everyone is as innocent as a child,
And no one behaves so cruel or wild.

Where one should care for earth, water, air, and nature,
And not a single act should go against their favor.
Where educated and uneducated, all should have
humanity,
And no one should be the victim of brutality.

Where our leaders should have wisdom, and their
decisions should be wise,
And their hearts should melt when the nation cries.

Where spending on health and education should be the
first priority,
And spending too much on showbiz should not be the
superiority.

Where love, care, and humility should day by day
increase,
And the world should know INDIA as a symbol of peace.

- Subi Sheikh

2. Mahakumbh: A Divine Gathering

Prayagraj, a land of cultural pride,
Celebrated Mahakumbh with faith as its guide.
Where Ganga, Yamuna, and Saraswati blend,
Millions arrived, their sins to mend.

With faith in hearts and prayers in mind,
The riverbanks shimmers, with lights divine.
Belief that one Amrit Snan cleanses within,
People toiled day and night, for hearts to win.

Chants of devotion filled the air,
Spreading faith beyond compare.
Despite the stampedes, the surging tide,
Spirituality stood strong with pride.

Thousands came from lands afar,
Braving struggles, following their stars.
Amidst the chaos, in moments dire,
Temples and mosques became their shelter and fire.

Belief in waters that heal and bless,
Pilgrims found peace in nature's caress.
Indeed, the river flows with a soothing sound,
A serenity nowhere else to be found.

Some found fortune, their earnings grew,
But how long would this wealth renew?
"Atithi Devo Bhava"—a truth we keep,
Yet some deceived , their promises weak.

Still, kindness shone, pure and bright,
Helping pilgrims embrace the light.
Now it's over —memories remain,
Some filled with joy, some with pain.

Keeping misleading voices aside,
People welcomed pilgrims with hearts open wide.
The streets lie silent, the banks now rest,
Life returns, putting faith to test.

Yet, as time flows and devotion remains,
Many will come, many will go—
But Sangam shall forever sustain.

- Subi Sheikh

3. The Beauty of Equality

I am a beautiful creation of nature,
All things turn in my favor.
I am one of a kind, beyond comparison,
Unique in my own version.

I am a man, stalwart with virility,
Not to be compared with a woman, graceful in
tranquility.
I am a woman, seraphic and luminous,
Not to be compared with a man, autonomous and
rigorous.

Both are distinctive, both admirable,
Each with responsibilities incomparable.
Then who raised the question of women's empowerment
—why?
Who declared that men must never cry?

Together, they balance nature, hand in hand,
Erasing competition, as one they withstand.

A woman is blessed to be a vivifier,
While a man is meant to be a sustainer.

No need for comparison—there is no reason,
For flowers bloom only when balance graces all seasons.
Both can feel shy, and both can fly,
With what they have, they should stand high.

A woman builds the society,
For a man to run with responsibility.
So lift each other with admiring support,
Keeping duties fair in proper rapport.

Today, a woman can be a matriarch,
Breaking the myth that household duties are her only
mark.
Men lead society, yes, it's true,
But women imbue it with strength anew.

None are perfect, none divine,
Let all stand together—let no one feel confined.
For both are equal, both significant, you see,
This is not a race for superiority, but harmony.

- Subi Sheikh

4. The Silent Cry of a Man

Once upon a time, there lived a man—
Strong and brave, making women, their slave.
Then came the term "Women Empowerment,"
Giving women wings to fly and making them brave.

The call for gender equality began to rise,
So they could work freely with men side by side.
Many struggled for this equality,
So they could rise without suffering brutality.

Laws were made to shield and defend,
To bring injustice to an end.
Yet, who knew some would misuse the same,
Turning justice into a mere game.

Oh dear! If you believe in gender equality,
Then stop demanding for alimony.
Otherwise, the voice of women's empowerment
Will all turn into baloney.

A man, too, plays many roles—
A son, a husband, a father, and more.
Balancing between parents and wife,
Indeed, it's not an easy chore.

Society's pressure of being a man,
Crushes him beneath its weight.
He cannot cry or show his pain,
For fear of judgment and silent hate.

Many men are also in pain,
Yet their voices go unheard again.
If they cry or speak their truth,
They are met with scorn and disdain.

You are your parents' princess, it's true,
And no doubt, he is their prince too.
You dream of a prince who loves, protects, and always
cares,
He, too, dreams of someone be always honest and fair.

Give him time to understand,
He may be slow but holds your hand.
He makes mistakes, though unaware,
Yet always tries to mend and repair.

Nobody sees his silent tears,

Hidden within his voice of fears.
He, too, learns things anew,
So how can he be perfect for you?

A cry that no one can see,
A silent cry—THE CRY OF A MAN.
His responsibilities overburden him,
Otherwise, he might have ran.

Yes, some men aren't good for society,
But so are some women with greed.
Laws should stand for truth and justice,
Not to favor one but serve all needs.

Proper investigation must be done,
Before declaring a man guilty.
For fairness must not wear a face,
But shine with truth and dignity.

- Subi Sheikh

5. The Unwritten Vow

Keeping the Almighty in mind, do you accept each other
as husband and wife?
Yes, I do, till eternal life.
Only one bond remains hereafter,
A sacred foundation, strong as a rafter.

Tying the knot, pledging as spouses,
Bound by some vows in sacred houses.
Yet some remain unwritten still—
Silent promises the heart fulfills.

Respect and care, both must show,
No interference from those we know.
When I feel low and burdens grow,
Your love should heal, your warmth should flow.

It is the expectation of the heart now—
Yes, it is the unwritten vow.

When tempers rise and patience fades,

Stand by my side as anger sways.
Through trials—be it health or gold,
Hold my hand; stay strong, be bold.

It is the expectation of the heart now—
Yes, it is the unwritten vow.

Responsibilities will surely come our way,
Let's divide the workload without delay.
If I stumble, fail, or fall,
Our bond must never break at all.

It is the expectation of the heart now—
Yes, it is the unwritten vow.

Our bond should not suffer from ego's rise,
We must stay together, no compromise.
I may not always get things right,
But finding-fault should not spark a fight.

It is the expectation of the heart now—
Yes, it is the unwritten vow.

This sacred bond, crafted by the Creator,
Loses its essence when one acts as a dictator.
It is a union of love, care, and affection,
And perfection should not be the expectation.

It is the expectation of the heart now—
Yes, it is the unwritten vow.

Equilibrium may waver with life's tides,
But gratitude should always reside.
Raising children is a shared duty,
Together, we must instill respect and beauty.

It is the expectation of the heart now—
Yes, it is the unwritten vow.

Selfless love, though left unsaid,
Should live in all the paths we tread.
Though vows are written, sealed, and signed,
The truest vows live in the mind.

It is an expectation of the heart now—
Yes, it is an unwritten vow.

- Subi Sheikh

6. The Bridge Between Generations

In my 30s, I sit with dreams and creation,
Lost in thoughts of time's swift transformation.
I come from an era of simple delights,
Where needs were few, and traditions felt right.

Peace filled our hearts as we welcomed all seasons,
Finding joy in small things without lavish reasons.
We lived with whatever we had,
Never longing for luxuries or trends gone mad.

Sundays meant cartoons, laughter, and cheer,
Not screens and trends that now appear.
Being alone filled us with fright,
Vacations at Grandma's were pure delight.

No shortcuts, no step-by-step guide,
We stumbled, we strived, we learned with pride.
Ambitions fueled our innocent dreams,
Unaware of the coming extremes.

Then came Gen Z—a wave so fast,
Bringing revolutions meant to last.
Revolutions of tech shaped their way,
Leaving millennials in awe and dismay.

Their curiosity moves at lightning speed,
Fueled by gadgets and digital need.
Now smartphones shape their every thought,
Books are forgotten, their wisdom distraught.

They have the tool—Apple and Android,
Yet fail to see emptiness in the void.
They swipe, they scroll, they follow the trends,
Validation now comes from virtual friends.

They don't realize their worth—this era is grand,
They are digital natives with knowledge in hand.
With tech, they can do wonders,
Many succeed, and their splendor thunders.

Information at their fingertips,
Yet wisdom often seems to slip.
They mock our struggle with tech's embrace,
But just wait—Gen Alpha sets the pace.

Born into AI, with hybrid aim,

They see the world through a different frame.
To some, they seem detached and naive,
Yet their era holds wonders we can't conceive.

With a blink, they soar beyond the moon,
Living in worlds where reality is strewn.
Metaverse dreams and digital streams,
Their universe flows beyond our means.

We claim their creativity is lost,
That tech has come at a greater cost.
But maybe, just maybe, they need a guide,
To balance both worlds side by side.

Each generation has its boon and bane,
Each unique in its own domain.
Instead of judgment, let's build a bridge,
Blending wisdom with innovation's edge.

Technology isn't the enemy here,
If used with purpose, not just veneer.
The past and future can coexist,
If we shape the world with a mindful twist.

- Subi Sheikh

7. Clock Vs. Me

Tick-tock, tick-tock,
Round the clock.
Time and tide wait for none.
Excuse me, who asked you?
Are you waiting just for fun?

Life is fun and mysterious.
Live it to the fullest, don't be too serious.
Dear clock, dear clock,
Don't let my schedule block.

You are at my service, not my boss.
All your hard work—yet no reward, what a loss!

Early in the morning at five, you ring.
See, I snooze you and sleep again—look, I win!
After ten minutes, I wake up as I wish.
Are you sad? Relax and cherish.

Rush! Rush! Rush! I must reach the office.

Are you playing tricks on me? Just behave.
You don't know that if I'm late,
"SORRY" is the word I save.

By evening, I return all tired.
I juggle tasks—shouldn't that be admired?
Doing just one job 24x7,
You don't even get a trophy!
Look at me, sitting relaxed with my coffee.

I take my time to cook dinner,
No need to be like you—a restless runner.
Oh, now it's my time to rest.
You go on, enjoy your running fest!

Life is a journey, it moves on and on,
Sometimes bright, sometimes drawn.
But what about you? You make people rush,
Chasing deadlines all day long.

Why are you always in such a hurry?
Because of you, the world is in a flurry.

Yet, I must thank you too,
For showing me every phase of life—
Childhood, youth, love, and parenthood thrive.
Now, as I lie on my deathbed,

It's time to step into eternity instead.

Oh, but wait—I've come back quick,
Slipped past the light with one last trick!
Not for wisdom, not for grace—
Just to ask... who took my place?!

Tick-tock, tick-tock,
Round the clock.

- Subi Sheikh

8. Education – A Legacy at Risk

Education is a must for all,
But it is at risk—it's a wake-up call.

Wake up today, or future generations will suffer,
They won't survive, for the competition is tougher.

It is good to have our religious faith,
But alongside, education leads life with grace.

"Money isn't everything, but we need money for
everything," is well said,
Yet earning by unfair means shows how much your soul
is dead.

Education shapes you better, setting you apart,
Guiding the mind, soul, and enriching the heart.

Educational institutes were once temples of learning,
But today, they have become mere sources of earning.

Even students are left with no virtues,
For neither schools nor homes have time to teach values.

Too many unnecessary holidays put education at risk,
We all await a proper plan that can fix it.

For every occasion celebrated in the city,
Schools are the first to close—it becomes a necessity.

Parents, on the other hand, push their own propaganda,
Turning education into a burdened enigma.

Pre-primary kids are considered too small for studies,
Primary students need "me time" because parents have
become their buddies.

Seniors lack basic concepts that should be clear,
Only a few excel, but such cases are rare.

Getting into college is the toughest race,
To reach that height, many competitions one must face.

Colleges have become expensive too,
For hefty taxes must be paid by both me and you.

Most of the youth take pride with allies,

Leaving education behind for political rallies.

Movies and media play their own game,
Diverting the youth toward directions of shame.

Distancing them from the world of education,
Multimedia plays a crucial role,
With the power to pull them into a black hole.

Education plus wisdom is the perfect combination,
Yet attaining both is difficult in this nation.

People have lost their sense of sensibility,
Media controls them, stripping away their thinking
ability.

But there is still time to fix this rolling disk,
For education and wisdom must unite—
To save education, a legacy still at risk.

- Subi Sheikh

9. Aura Of Women

Mirror, Mirror on the Wall
Which woman is the most beautiful of all?

The mirror said, "All are beautiful and all are unique,
And the strength of women is beyond mystique."

So be a woman with technology and advancement,
Enlighten yourself—stop begging for empowerment.
You have your own aura, you were born empowered,
Never doubt yourself, you are strong and admired.

Live a life full of grace,
Don't chase things that aren't your place.
Try your best to maintain relationships,
But if they turn toxic, don't endure that hardship.

You are the most precious creation of the world—
A daughter, a wife, a mother—you are a pearl.
Don't change your face with artificial things,
You are a masterpiece, embrace your wings.

You are the queen of your home, without you, it's just a
house.
Your multitasking begins the moment you rouse.
You may not always receive love, care, or affection,
But the One who created you holds you in high
appreciation.

He knew you could care for all His creations,
So He made you with utmost dedication.

So dear woman, Stop feeling pity for yourself,
Even if you're hurt, rise—know your wealth.

Stop believing the mirror all the time,
Just be you, and let your light shine.

- Subi Sheikh

10. Give Them Wings Not Their Hues

Overprotecting a child—from crying, from falling, from
pain,
Shielding them always—what do they gain?
Upbringing them with a golden spoon,
Do you think this is parenting, or just a cocoon?

Childhood—a time to explore and grow,
Yet lullabies fade, their echoes low.
From the first breath, screens take control,
Parenting is lost in the digital scroll.

If the child cries, a mobile soothes,
They don't realize it's a silent noose.
A virtual cage, a glowing screen,
Where real emotions go unseen.

Parents rush at their every call,
Cushioning each and every fall.
'No' is a word they never hear,

Yet the real world won't always cheer.

Life has switched from books to screens,
Empty playgrounds—nowhere to be seen.
Bound in sugar-coated chains,
Unprepared for life's real pains.

For every small thing, schools take the blame,
For every setback, parents complain.
Forgetting that values start at home,
Now, disrespect has freely grown.

They build castles high in the sky,
Proud their child speaks bold and sly.
But when their voice turns into a shout,
Control is lost—there's no way out.

Some parents, on the other side,
Hold too tight, with love as a guide.
A golden cage, a rigid plan,
A life controlled by a steadfast hand.

They never let their child explore,
Silver platters, dreams ignored.
Safe in storms, yet lost in calm,
In overprotection, they lose their charm.

They must fall to rise again,
Face the storm, endure the rain.
Let them stumble, let them choose,
Give them wings, but not their hues.

Dear parents, you shape the age,
Your love must guide, not just cage.
Teach them wisdom, let them fly,
Let them fail, let them try.

Don't let the essence of parenthood fade,
Our children are the future—
They have milestones to brave.

- Subi Sheikh

11. Unchain Your Soul

In every stage of life, we wonder—what is life's goal?
Every time, we struggle for our awakening soul.
Too many ifs and buts, pros and cons,
Burdened with society's norms.
How do we find peace in this mental storm?
Stay calm, take control — unchain your soul.

As a child, you're taught to obey,
But values shift from place to place each day.
In front of guests, you must be polite,
Or risk being judged, with no defense in sight.
Stay calm, take control — unchain your soul.

In teenage years, the pressure grows,
To score, excel, and stay composed.
How you sit, stand, speak, or act—
All are measured, all are tracked.
And with no guide to clear the way,
You're left to struggle, come what may.
Stay calm, take control — unchain your soul.

Then comes the stage of choosing a life partner,
But it's as difficult as finding a skilled gardener.
Even if you're happily bound forever,
Society tests your bond with endless endeavor.
Stay calm, take control — unchain your soul.

If you are a girl, you are buried under taunts.
I agree— even at night they haunt.
And if you're a boy, the weight you bear,
Provider, protector—life seems unfair.
Stay calm, take control — unchain your soul.

After crossing so many hurdles in life,
Even in life's final stride,
A property fight may still decide.
Stay calm, take control — unchain your soul.

But through it all, one truth remains—
Contentment frees you from these chains.
No rule, no voice should cloud your way,
Embrace yourself—come what may.

Stay calm, take control — unchain your soul.

- Subi Sheikh

12. The Diet That Starts Tomorrow

All trouble aside, losing weight is the real fight
Even if you eat nothing, you keep on gaining—it's
absolutely right.
Once upon a time, when I was in my twenties,
Slim, trim, beautiful—weighing just in the forties.

Then I got married, happily ever after,
Unaware that body weight would be my next chapter.
Eating delicious food freely, day and night
Fifty-five on the weighing scale gave me a fright.

Now, I decided to diet and exercise from tomorrow.
Woke up with an omelette, my favorite—"Let's eat now
and then feel sorrow."
Rajma, chawal, and lunch, I somehow resist,
But my child left food that I had to finish.

Evening came, I controlled and did not munch.
But a guest is like a God—with them, I had to crunch.
Dinner seemed easy to avoid,
Until my husband brought golgappe and rasmalai—I was
overjoyed!

My portion would go to waste, so I had to consume.
Diet? Let it be tomorrow—I will resume.

The next day, there was a demand for different parathas,
So breakfast, I had to modify.
I made them all but didn't eat—
Tell me, how is that justified?

Since I started dieting, my Insta reels conspire,
Showing only delicious food to fuel my desire.
How to control my tongue? It's a serious struggle.
Balancing diet and cravings is like learning to juggle.

Then, I took an oath at home,
"I won't diet when I roam."
I enjoyed my vacations cheating diet a little bit,

But my weighing scale did not like it.

Every day, different delicious dishes I swallow,
Thinking, "I will diet from tomorrow."
Vegetarian food has its own taste, the taste of nature,
While biryani, kebabs, and roasted chicken have their
own flavor.

I found myself sitting, surrounded by these tasty meals,
Wishing I could taste them all—just by watching them in
reels.
It is beyond my control to stick to my diet.
My family stares at me when I eat—
I stare back and stay quiet.

They laugh at me for not completing my wishes.
"How can one walk away from such tempting dishes?"
I listed only a few—
South Indian, Mughlai, and Continental are cuisines
never-ending and new.

Then, I surrendered my diet plan,

And stopped looking at those diet-conscious clans.
The trend of using the weighing scale, I will no longer
follow,
Yet, every day, I reassure my heart—
"I will start my diet from tomorrow!"

- Subi Sheikh

13. Saving The Planet Only On Paper

The serene magic of wildlife and trees,
Capturing moments in standing peaks and dancing seas,
Mysteries hidden in clouds and stars—
A glimpse of their beauty heals all scars.

Each day, the sun adores the earth,
Rising with a golden kiss,
Unveiling the planet's splendor without a miss.
Each evening, it embraces the world and sets apart,
Only to rise again the next morning and restart.

But now, the earth cries, pleading for aid,
While humans chase wealth and let nature degrade.
Deforestation spreads at its peak,
Leaving the soil severed, its roots now weak.

The use of plastics is banned on paper,
Yet factories run in humans' favor.
Tons of garbage flood rivers and seas,

While pledges to save them remain signed and freeze.

April 22 is Earth Day worldwide,
Spreading awareness, a moment of pride.
Yet it's confined to statuses and fleeting charts,
Like waves that vanish before they start.
Similarly, Wildlife, Water, and Ocean Day—
Marked on calendars, then forgotten away.

But shouldn't saving and respecting nature
Be an everyday act, a part of our stature?
During lockdown, when humans were confined,
Flora and fauna found peace; nature realigned.
We saw nature heal and reclaim its space,
Yet we continue to plunder without a trace.

The truth is—nature doesn't need us; we need it.
Yet we exploit it without care, not even a bit.
Save soil, water, air and the Earth.
Don't just shout; prove your worth.
Play your part in restoring nature with pride,
For a thriving Earth should not remain only on paper but
worldwide.

- Subi Sheikh

14. Footprints Of My Good Deeds

Favors fade, forgotten with ease—so mean.
The footprints of my good deeds remain unseen.

At work, they ask for my time and skill,
Needing my help, I give with goodwill.
But when I seek them in my hour of need,
They vanish, like whispers in the breeze.

My heart moves to help out of empathy,
Yet their favors feel like selfish generosity.

I stand by my family, always on call,
Yet when I stumble, they let me fall.
I give my all—yet when I despair,
They offer mere words, as if unaware.

People spare no chance to put me down,
Some degrade me with a public frown.

Be it a family function or an office task,
I paint each detail with colors that last.
Yet when it's time for appreciation,
Others take the credit—my efforts lost also in narration.

The work I complete, through endless nights,
Goes unnoticed, though their smallest acts shine bright.

I give my share with love and grace,
Yet betrayal meets me, face to face.

They pile their burdens onto my back,
Then gossip freely behind my track.

I keep on giving, never slowing,
Yet my heart wonders—where is it all going?

Favors fade, forgotten with ease—so mean.
The footprints of my good deeds remain unseen.

Still, I hold faith deep in my heart,
Knowing One above records every part.
One day, He will listen and see,
Rewarding the striving of my soul eternally.

- Subi Sheikh

15. The Battle Of Who Is Right

Many battles have been fought in history,
Yet their reasons remain a mystery.

Everyone holds their own belief,
But these differences shatter peace,
Turning power into ruthless grief.

In every argument, ego takes the stage,
A silent war fueled by pride and rage.
And in this battle, fierce and tight,
It's never easy to decide—who is right?

This clash of right and wrong tears bonds apart,
No one bends—each demands the greater part.
Families divide over wealth and land,
Yet no one extends a healing hand.

Teenagers wrestle with choices unknown,
A second battle rages as they grow.

Decades pass, yet nothing fades,
The generation war in different shades.

Victory doesn't always belong to the just,
For arguments breed endless dust.
And when the dust begins to settle,
Who truly wins this futile battle?

"Who is right?"—a question untold,
A puzzle endless, weary, and cold.
For those who try to make it right,
It's an exhausting, endless fight.

Imagine a world free from this strife,
Where hearts embrace a peaceful life.
No walls of ego, no lines drawn,
Only harmony from dusk till dawn.

Acceptance blooms where kindness stays,
No pain, no tears—just brighter days.
A world where love and smiles unite,
Ending the battle of "Who is right?"

- Subi Sheikh

16. Indian Elections: The Grand Deception Show

India, a land so rich, so free,
A beacon of vast democracy.
Now the time has come to see,
Leaders should rise by merit and degree.

Festivals shine, one by one,
Yet none as grand when elections come.
Rallies march from street to street,
With cunning hawks and hungry fleets.

What starts with slogans, bold and bright,
Ends in chaos, fear, and fight.
Tension grips the suffering folk,
While banners rise and people choke.

Posters rise on every wall,
Their cost beyond what most can call.
Some people seem so free, so proud,
And dance like puppets in the crowd.

Millions spent to buy the vote,
Supporters fade—just floaters gloat.
Promises false, yet hopes so high,
Disguised within a well-planned lie.

Ballots fade like stories old,
EVM tricks are easily sold.
Voters stand with dreams so grand,
Yet polling booths stay in their hands.

Holi, Diwali—all combined,
In victory's fire, the blind will find.
Yet history shows no promise stays,
They vanish in the winner's ways.

The losers scream, they cry, they blame,
Forgetting they once played the same game.
One is bad, the other worse,
Power fuels an endless thirst.

Some ignite the flames of price,
Some divide through faith's device.
The public plays the biggest fool,
Thinking leaders make them cool.

Yet, they pay the heaviest price,

Through silent tax and sacrifice.
Media plays its dirty game,
Hiding truth without a shame.

Development left in endless queue,
Public funds are misused too.
Speak a word—you'll face the cost,
Home and family might be lost.

The rich grow richer every year,
The poor sink deeper into fear.
While leaders tour in grand display,
On public's money, they fly away.

Corruption stands in broad daylight,
Fake degrees, yet they hold might.
They rule by caste, by creed, by name,
Dividing hearts, yet feel no shame.

India fades in false disguise,
As WhatsApp grants its own degrees wise.
Until we break this endless flow,
This land will never truly grow.
As long as fools still play along,
Elections sing their Deception Song.

- Subi Sheikh

17. The Fading Light Of Education

Gone are the days when books were our best friends,
Now, knowledge is just a click away; it all depends.

Education is fading in every corner,
And an educated person is left with no honor.

Dancing and media influencing have become a game,
Everyone chases them for money, glory, and fame.

Sense of humor has turned so cheap,
While respect, honor, love, and affection lie in a heap.

Language is losing its beauty and grace,
As leaders divide it, giving it a religious face.

But language is a bridge that connects hearts,
Embrace the new, and let unity starts.

Very few now keep education their first priority,

While others chase wealth to flaunt superiority.

No matter how much you earn or own,
Educate yourself to grow and be known.

Learn your religious values with clarity,
For they help a nation rise with morality.

Education is the greatest tool of all,
It shapes your soul and helps you stand tall.

Dear parents, you are blessed and wise,
With all the means to help your children rise.

Make them smart, strong, and kind,
Teach them faith and knowledge combined.

"Education is a tool of success"—someone once said it
right,
For it makes you human, filling life with light.

- Subi Sheikh

18. Life Keeps Getting Cheaper

The price of guns grows steeper,
While life keeps getting cheaper.

Nine months in a mother's womb,
The pain of labor—
Apart from women, none can assume.
This is truly a sad reality,
Society is losing morality.
Anger and anxiety are spreading rife,
People give no second thought before taking life.
Reasons? Trivial—junk, love, or pride,
A drunken rage, a wounded side.

They give no thought to their dirty will,
Age doesn't matter—They just rape and kill.
In domestic violence, she may still persist,
But death for dowry—how can it be missed?
Hatred takes root in poisoned ground,
A property dispute—another life drowned.

Drunk on power, high on pride,
They speed through streets, fate cast aside.
Metal crashes, sirens wail—
A careless act, a tragic tale.
Proposals of love, if they don't crack,
Are reason enough for an acid attack.
Values lost, conscience numb,
Even a child can wield a gun.

For every small thing, it's easy to take a life.
Love, care, affection, and pain for others no longer
survive.
No one takes responsibility for these precious lives,
Their greed and ego kill humans like flies.
The ones who mourn know sorrow's weight,
An emptiness even time cannot abate.

The price of guns grows steeper,
While life keeps getting cheaper.

- Subi Sheikh

19. The Rise of My Little Girl: Wings of My Heart

India—a land where hearts still ache,
Where a girl's birth some celebrate, some fake.
I too once followed that old-time trend,
But my reasons? A little different, my friend.

I wished my firstborn would be a boy,
An elder brother, your tasks to deploy.
But when they whispered, "It's a girl," my hopes fell low,
For now, my little one had to stand on her own.

Yet, when I held you, my sorrow erased,
Like rain reviving land long unfazed.
Every giggle, every tiny feat,
Turned life's rhythm into a melody sweet.

From first steps to birthday cheer,
I planned each moment, held you near.
Forgive me, my love, for times I sighed,
Loneliness made me a mother who tried.

I scolded, I guided, I pushed you to grow,
Not out of anger, but love, you should know.
Your little face, puffed up in rage,
Still, I stood firm—your life's sage.

You grumbled, stumbled, yet soared so high,
Each triumph of yours lit up my sky.
From chessboard wins to debate stage glow,
You gave me goosebumps—I want you to know.

Time slips by, like a blink of an eye,
Yet my prayers for you still touch the sky.
Now, teenage years knock at our door,
A challenge for me, yet I fear it no more.

I hover, I spy—yes, I admit,
Annoying, frustrating, but I won't quit.
Academics, debates,chess or music beats,
No matter the dream, I'm there in the seats.

I recall the letter you once wrote,
Listing my flaws in every note.
Now, you laugh and hug me tight,
Those moments turn my dark to light.

Each hug of yours, my heart's delight,

Yet when you're sad, I lose my night.
Gracefully, you rise, strong and proud,
Always shining beyond the crowd.

Your father—reserved, yet fierce for you,
His love, though silent, is deep and true.
The future is unknown, unwritten, unplanned,
But your strength will make it truly grand.

With love, I raised you, taught you to be wise,
With faith in your heart and dreams in your eyes.
Be patient, be kind, let wisdom stay,
For home and religion will light your way.

So dream, my love, with courage bright,
Stand tall, be bold, embrace your light.
Live fully, love deeply, be fearless, stay kind,
And leave a mark on every mind.

- Subi Sheikhi

20. The Silence of the World

A mother was singing to her child—
A lullaby.
Constant surveillance and airstrikes
Forced her to say goodbye.

People once lived with laughter and cheer,
Unaware that destruction was near.
No one knew their echoes and cries
Would be buried beneath shattered skies.

The sound of aircraft fills them with fear,
For bombs are all they ever hear.
The city crumbles, torn apart,
Washed away like a work of art.

Their nights are haunted, their days the same,
Airstrikes roaring in endless shame.
Missiles fall on schools, on care—
No place is safe, no life is spared.

A mother wails, her son lies cold.
A child with no one left to hold.
The stars still shine in the darkened sky,
While on the ground, the children cry.

Palestine and Gaza weep in vain,
Wounds too deep, scars remain.

Innocents tortured, imprisoned, confined,
Hearts so hateful, mercy declined.
Even their bread, their hope denied,
Yet still, they stand—uncrushed inside.

A small child sobs,
"To Allah, I will complain."
If He asked what you had done,
How would you explain?

Genocide has left the land in despair,
Nothing remains—
But faith in the air.

They burn the land, reduce it to dust,
Yet their spirits rise—
Resilient and just.

Now is the time—the world must speak.

No longer can we stay so meek.
But oh, I forgot—
The world turns blind, the world plays dumb.
Their greed and power
Have left them numb.

They watch the suffering, hear the cries,
Yet silence lingers as justice dies.
And if you can't do much,
Then take a stand, boycott, and prove—
That even in silence, you disapprove.

And if you think this is just another war,
Then wait—one day, it knocks at your door.

This is not about religion or creed,
Not Hindu, Muslim, Jew, or Christian, indeed.
Raise your voice against genocide's flood,
For this is a matter of human blood.

- Subi Sheikh

21. Whispers In The Ink

Owning the power of words like royalty,
A poet's ink, laced with rhetoric, whispers with loyalty.

Thoughts whisper softly in silent embrace,
Yet on paper, they rise—a voice to displace.

I bleed ink, not blood, yet it runs deep,
A force of revolution, a storm that won't sleep.

I find beauty in leaves, withered and dry,
Nature consoles me beneath the vast sky.

But my heart bleeds to witness nature's plight, Awaken,
dear humans—restore its light.

My heart bleeds for souls suffering in pain,
Be a healer, dear humans—let kindness reign.

My heart bleeds to see corruption and greed's wave,
Hold virtue and truth, dear humans, and fear your grave.

My imagination knows no bound—
Soaring above, diving below the ground.

I seek not war, but a revolution of peace, Through ink, I
whisper—let turmoil cease.

Ink holds power, as history has shown,
It echoes in time, in voices well-known.

Whispers in ink—don't take them light,
For words of peace can end a fight.

The weight of words cannot be measured, Yet in the
heart, they remain forever treasured.

- Subi Sheikh

9 789369 536450